5

Powerful Questions for Coaching, Mentoring, and Leading at Work

555
Powerful Questions for Coaching, Mentoring, and Leading at Work

The Art of Asking Powerful Questions to Unlock Potential, Improve Performance and Empower Others

Be.Bull Publishing Group
Mauricio Vasquez
Toronto, Canada

Authors:

Be.Bull Publishing Group
Mauricio Vasquez
First Printing: January 2022

ISBN-978-1-7779531-7-1

Author

Hi. I'm Mauricio Vasquez, and I'd love to share a little about myself with you. I'm a dynamic professional who's passionate about personal development, professional growth, and positively impacting people's lives.

Throughout my career, I've had the opportunity to work in various fields, including risk management, insurance, e-commerce, and coaching, where I've applied my skills and expertise to create lasting change for individuals and organizations alike.

I'm the proud founder and co-owner of Aria Capri International Inc., an e-commerce company on a mission to enhance the lives and wellbeing of professionals and families. Additionally, I support mining, power, and renewable energy companies by offering risk management and insurance solutions that enable them to safeguard their corporate value, reach their potential, and contribute positively to the environment and surrounding communities.

Besides that, I'm a dedicated professional and life coach. In my coaching practice, I collaborate with fellow professionals, helping them achieve better outcomes, lead more fulfilling lives, and become more engaged, effective individuals. I wholeheartedly believe in the transformative power of asking insightful questions to unlock our potential and propel us forward.

In my personal life, I'm passionate about entrepreneurship, marketing, continuous learning, maintaining a healthy lifestyle, mindfulness, and meditation. I currently live in Toronto, Canada, with my wonderful wife Devon and our charming daughter Aria Capri.

I hope this book provides you with inspiration and guidance as you embark on your own journey toward personal and professional growth. Enjoy!

Mauricio Vasquez
MBA, B.Eng, M.Mktg, ERM, CRM, CIP, ATC

PS. As a token of appreciation, I'd like to provide you with a FREE copy of my book as PDF and EPUB format. Just scan the QR codes shown below.

PDF Format

EPUB Format

Dear Valued Reader

I'd like to please kindly ask you to leave me a review on Amazon. I don't have the same budget as big publishing companies, so your input would be really appreciated.

To leave your review of this book, please scan this QR code, and it will take you directly to Amazon's review section.

Your support will mean a lot to me, and I thank you in advance for your help!

Mauricio

Unlock Your Leadership Potential with Artificial Intelligence

I am excited to offer you exclusive access to a transformative tool, *My Coaching, Mentoring & Leadership Advisor GPT*, developed with OpenAI's ChatGPT technology. This advanced Artificial Intelligence tool enhances your interaction with ChatGPT, offering a more tailored and responsive experience.

This custom GPT (Generative Pre-trained Transformer) model is expertly crafted to provide targeted help in leadership, coaching, and mentoring.

As a dynamic Artificial Intelligence companion, it aligns with your unique professional style and needs, providing tailored advice and insights to help navigate your leadership path.

Engaging with this GPT is incredibly intuitive, and simpler than you might expect. Once you access to ChatGPT, you'll be greeted by a user-friendly interface where you can input your questions or prompts.

My Coaching, Mentoring & Leadership Advisor
Enhancing your leadership and growth through expert AI-powered coaching, mentoring and leadership guidance to make a positive impact in others and yourself.
By Aria Capri International Inc.

The GPT responds almost instantly, offering valuable insights and guidance.

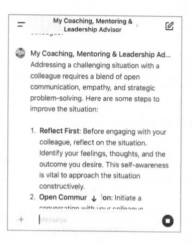

Whether you aim to enhance your leadership abilities, improve team dynamics, or foster personal and professional growth, *My Coaching, Mentoring & Leadership Advisor GPT* stands as your gateway to innovative professional development.

In these pics, you can see the user interface you'll encounter when accessing 'My Coaching, Mentoring & Leadership Advisor' GPT. This visual reference provides a clear preview of what to expect, guiding you through your first steps in utilizing this innovative tool.

To start your journey towards advanced leadership and coaching skills, scan this QR code.

INTRODUCTION

Asking questions is, has been and always will be part of our nature. Questions allow us to gather information, learn new things, and strengthen our relationships with others in unique ways.

Why is asking powerful and insightful questions important for your work and life?

Foremost, asking questions and really listening to others shows that you truly care. When you are at work, and you ask powerful questions to your colleagues, they will then know that you value them and care about their needs and opinions. Your interactions with them will always be more successful and gratifying when you are honest and intentional in acknowledging their actual needs and knowledge gaps.

Asking questions will allow you to align your or your organization's goals with your colleagues' objectives, priorities, and needs. This needs to be done with understanding and empathy towards others. You may have a general idea of what your colleagues want from you and your company, including the goals they're trying to achieve, or what needs they are trying to satisfy. However, it is never that easy.

What if you are making wrong assumptions and have false beliefs, and as a result, your words and actions are not really in line with what your colleagues are thinking and feeling? This is a recipe for ineffective relationships and performance.

Although no one can really argue the value of powerful questions, how often do you pose meaningful questions to your colleagues and teammates? what questions are you asking? are you using the right terminology? are you asking too many close-ended questions? and finally, are you using the answers to help strengthen your relationships or help others improve their awareness and performance? This one last question is key. If you are asking questions, and not doing anything with the responses, what is the point? It can create the opposite result you are trying to achieve. Asking questions goes far beyond exchanging information.

Here is a quote I find very relevant to asking the right questions:

"*The tough thing is figuring out what questions to ask, but once you do that, the rest is really easy.*" Elon Musk.

There is no need to come up with counterproductive questions or even spend hours trying to figure out the much-needed powerful questions. I have done all the heavy lifting for you.

This book has 555 powerful questions for coaching, mentoring, and leading at work. This book will help you ask questions—and particularly, asking the right questions that will draw out insightful answers — answers can help you transform your business.

GUIDELINES FOR ASKING POWERFUL QUESTIONS

Read the following guidelines to learn more about asking powerful questions that unlock learning and improve performance.

- **Effective questions are open or focused, depending on the context:** Questions that open awareness and learning are open-ended questions that cannot be answered with a yes or no. Such questions evoke deeper thinking and reflection.

- **Effective questions support learning:** You want to stimulate thinking and deepen your colleagues' understanding of what is going on. Hence, your insightful questions need to help focus your colleagues' attention on those aspects of the issue or situation you or they are dealing with that are most valuable.

- **Effective questions are asked for the benefit of others:** The intent is for the question to stimulate your colleagues' thinking and to deepen their understanding. It is not necessarily about you and what you want.

- **Effective questions engage a personal response:** Work is about results, and it is people who create results. Your job as a manager and leader is to engage colleagues by inviting a personal response–how they feel, what emotions they are bringing to the situation. The more a question invites a personal response to a challenge or choice, the more powerful it is for facilitating learning.

- **Effective questions look beyond problems to future outcomes:** When a colleague is entangled in a problem, impactful questions shift the perspective from the problem to the solution and will open new opportunities for action.

- **Effective questions facilitate openness versus defensiveness:** Impactful questions are worded and expressed with a non–judgmental tone and with open body language to prevent a defensive reaction. It is usually best to avoid questions that begin with "why" since they elicit defensive responses or explanations.

- **Effective questions co-create best options versus manipulating outcomes:** Impactful questions are not intended to manipulate or lead colleagues to the option you might think is the best option. If you want to suggest, it is best made directly as a suggestion versus a disguised directive through a question.

- **Less is more:** For powerful questions, less is usually more. Ask only one question at a time and avoid long-winded, complicated questions. A short, simple question–What is that all about? What will the consequences be? - This pulls the client straight to the core.

TIPS FOR THE USE OF THIS BOOK

- We split questions into different chapters, depending on the type of question. Use this as a reference only. Many questions, if not all, could fall into two or three categories.
- The best approach for any meaningful conversation is by listening. Listening to what the person you are with has to say with his/her words, emotions, physical expressions, and energy.
- For better results, tailor the questions to the specific conversation and colleague you are having a conversation with.
- Combine the questions as you see fit to produce deeper insights.
- Some questions come with a couple of options to tailor them and with a blank third option to spark your creativity and come up with your own unique question.
- Asking follow-up questions is a great way to dive deeper into the conversation and uncover what really matters.
- Questions need to be tailored to the specific conversation you are having.
- Adapt the questions to your own vocabulary.
- Ask only one question at a time, and avoid long-winded, complicated questions.

Table of Contents

Accountability

1	How can you enforce your sense of accountability towards (yourself/your responsibilities/_____)?
2	How can you help yourself stay accountable to your (goals/commitments/_____)?
3	What can you do to be more fully present with your (colleagues/supervisor/_____)?
4	How do you want to hold yourself accountable?
5	Who can you ask to hold you accountable?
6	How would you like others to hold you accountable?
7	What is the plan to keep yourself on track?
8	What can you help yourself be more courageous?
9	What do you want to acknowledge yourself for?
10	What relationships can you use as an accountability measure?

Action

11	What actions will you take towards your (purpose/learning goals/_____) this week?
12	What specific actions are you prepared to take to get (new clients/customers/_____)?
13	What is the plan for you to achieve your (objectives/competitive edge/_____)?
14	What is the next step to complete your (business plan/marketing strategy/_____)?
15	What is there for you to (manage/control/_____)?
16	How do you manage your (suppliers/subordinates/_____)?
17	What have you tried so far with (investors/contractors/_____) to improve the situation?
18	What will you do differently at work based on what you have discovered about (yourself/others/_____)?

19	What do you need to do less of to get closer to your (quota/team/_____)?
20	What is the most important (task/project/_____) to act on now?
21	What is the first step you want to take to reduce (variable costs/outstanding payments/_____)?
22	What should you continue to do to maintain a healthy relationship with (colleagues/suppliers/_____)?
23	Which factors are most vital in taking a (proactive approach/bold step/_____)?
24	How can you inspire yourself to shift your viewpoints to find new opportunities for action?
25	How can you achieve the accomplishment you want for your future?

Awareness

26	What are you becoming more aware of about yourself and your (work/work ethic/_____)?
27	What do you love about your (role/position/_____)?
28	What do you secretly dread at work?
29	What is true for you right now about your (job prospects/professional progression/_____)?
30	Where are you over-invested or under-invested in your work?
31	What would you like to get out of this (exercise/experience/_____)?
32	What is clearer now about your (priorities/competencies/_____)?
33	Who are you becoming when you are being (selfish/mindful/_____)?

34	What is your current reality?
35	Are you in a down-spiral or positive mindset?
36	How is the (mission/vision/_____) of the company influencing your pattern of thinking?
37	When you say you are not ready, what image or picture comes to your mind?
38	What image or picture do you see in your mind when you talk about (value proposition/pain points/_____) of the company?
39	Where your ideal and real self are similar?
40	Where your ideal and real self are different?
41	What questions do you have about the (culture/mission/_____) of the company?

42	What are you becoming more aware of about (yourself/your team/_____)?
43	How can you continue to stay aware of the impact of your thoughts on your (responsibilities/role/_____)?
44	What do you want to acknowledge yourself for regarding your contribution to the (company/team/_____)?
45	What do you imagine is going on here?
46	What is at stake if you don't reach your (sales target/key performance indicators/_____)?
47	What is required to help you raise your awareness of underlying (beliefs/assumptions/_____)?
48	How can you raise your awareness about the (beliefs/assumptions/_____) you are operating with and of the consequences of operating with them?
49	How can you help yourself notice your emotions, both the ones you express and the ones that lie beneath what you are saying?

50	What (meaning/interpretation/_____) are you placing on your team's feedback?
51	What new awareness do you have because of not achieving the desired (outcome/solution/_____) you had in mind?
52	What is missing from the (action plan/process/_____)?
53	What do you notice about the (client/yourself/_____)?
54	What assumptions have you made in the past that were proven to be false?
55	How can you uncover any internal and external obstacles in executing your actions?

Belief

56	Where are you in balance or out of balance with your (workload/commitments/_____)?
57	What are the pieces of evidence for your thinking about the (business plan/strategy/_____)?
58	What are counter-evidences for your thinking the (business plan/strategy/_____)?
59	What beliefs do you have that empower you to finish your (goals/commitments/_____)?
60	What beliefs do you have that disempower yourself from fulfilling your (goals/commitments/_____)?
61	How your (beliefs/work ethic/_____) shape your actions?
62	What beliefs or assumptions about you are being challenged?
63	What assumptions are you making about the (situation/audience/_____)?

64	What is it about the (situation/challenge/_____) that could give you the outcome you want?
65	How well does the belief that you hold about the (issue/problem/_____) serve you?
66	How helpful is it to you to believe that your work can't (improve/change/_____)?
67	How helpful is it to you to believe that work should always be fair?
68	How helpful is it to you to believe that there is another way of looking at the (issue/problem/_____) that might serve you better?
69	How helpful is it to you to believe that there could be a different outcome in terms of how you feel about the (issue/problem/_____)?
70	What disturbs you most?
71	What do you have to lose?

72	Who are you at your best?
73	What beliefs or assumptions are you making about (yourself/others/_____)?
74	Where do your assumptions or beliefs limit you?
75	What are the implications of your (proposal/responses/_____)?
76	What beliefs about work prevent you from moving forward?
77	How else can you think about your (behavior/attitude/_____)?
78	How can you shift your underlying (beliefs/assumptions/_____)?
79	Who do you want to become?

80	How do you know the (proposed solution/proposed time/_____) works?
81	What don't you believe today that you believed to be true a long time ago?
82	What are your perspectives on your (responsibilities/motivation/_____)?
83	What if you really believed that you could change your (career/performance/_____) by changing your choices?

Challenge

84	Where do you want to go with the (thought/conversation/_____)?
85	How can you motivate yourself to do something that is outside of your comfort zone?
86	What is a new challenge you want to work on?
87	What does need to be clarified more?
88	Where are you off-track in your (career/project/_____)?
89	What gets in your way?
90	What do you need to do differently to be a more positive influence on your (teammates/clients/_____)?
91	What choices do you make about your own identity?

92	In what ways does your (negativity/mindset/_____) serve you?
93	What else do you see when you see a (problem/difficulty/_____)?
94	What will be the process to help you move into a different frame of reference?
95	What data can you select that could refute your assumptions?
96	What are you being challenged by with (public speaking/team projects/_____)?
97	What will be more challenging for you than your current (role/responsibilities/_____)?
98	What do you see as the obstacles in your (way/professional life/_____)?
99	What will you do about the (challenge/obstacle/_____)?

100	How do you best navigate through a (challenge/obstacle/_____)?
101	How do you best adapt to a new (challenge/position/_____)?
102	How do you best thrive in a new (role/position/_____)?
103	What alternative view is there for you to look at on the (situation/argument/_____)?
104	What strengths can you draw on to help you deal with the (challenge/project/_____)?
105	What internal resistance do you have to taking action?
106	What about now?
107	How can you help yourself see things from a different perspective?

108	What does it get in the way?
109	What was an experience where you took a risk and it paid off?
110	What is the limit of your comfort zone?
111	What did it impede your (goals/work/_____)?

Change

112	How can you help yourself shift to a more effective mindset?
113	What do you need to do to improve (customer service/defect rate/_____)?
114	Where in the (sales process/client service process/_____) are you most stuck?
115	What did work about the (situation/project/_____)?
116	What did not work about the (situation/project/_____)?
117	What would it be like if the (challenge/problem/_____) were solved?
118	What shifts in perspective do you need to make?
119	If you could change your (work/team/_____), how would you change it?

120	How would your work be different tomorrow because of what you do today?
121	What can you change?
122	What would you do if you wanted to change your (work routine/attitude/_____)?
123	What would be the impact if you do not change your (work/routine/_____)?
124	What shift in (thinking/attitude/_____) do you need to make?
125	What do you need to let go of?
126	Where are your areas of continued development?
127	What is the change you want to see in (yourself/the team/_____)?

Commitment

128	What will have to happen for you to act on your (responsibilities/vision/_____)?
129	What are you responsible for in the upcoming (prospecting meeting/team meeting/_____)?
130	What are you committed to (achieving/sharing/_____)?
131	What will you put in place to support your (commitment/work/_____)?
132	What do you commit to do to get a (promotion/salary increase/_____)?
133	How committed are you to move forward with the new (project/responsibilities/_____)?
134	How are you going to hold yourself to the commitment?
135	How can you stay in control?

Creativity

136	What do you want to do as a (next project/role/_____) at work?
137	How can you discover more enjoyable ways to accomplish what you need to accomplish?
138	What lines of questioning or paths of exploration would you take for yourself?
139	What do you have when your creativity is unleashed?
140	How does your creativity get unleashed?
141	What connections do you see between your (performance/habits/_____) and your (fulfillment/balanced scorecard/_____)?
142	How would you describe your (role/contribution/_____) to others?
143	What is important about being creative with others?
144	How do you create a relationship of trust with (yourself/clients/_____)?
145	What is the value of accessing your creative source?
146	How do you connect with the source of your creativity?

Decisions

147	What is a realistic time frame for you to accomplish your (performance goals/tasks/_____)?
148	How do you manage your (time/prioritize tasks/_____)?
149	What new possibilities for action do you see with your (team/supervisor/_____)?
150	What is going to be most important to you about the decision to (rescind/join/_____)?
151	What do you most want from the decision to (rescind/join/_____)?
152	How does your choice to (take part/join/_____) allow you to express your values?
153	What are you willing to do to (win market share/build volume sales/_____)?
154	How can you better balance your open mind and critical reflection to make the best choices you could make?
155	What will you focus your (energy/time/_____) on moving forward?
156	How are you bringing yourself to (work/team meetings/_____)?

Excitement

157	How do you best develop yourself?
158	What excites you the most about (management/leadership/_____)?
159	What do you feel most energized by?
160	When you have a (promotion/salary increase/_____), what will that give you on a deep level?
161	What would make your (work/relationships with others/_____) more satisfying for you?
162	In what situations is your energy going up?
163	What would be the reason for your energy going (up/down/_____)?
164	In what situations is your energy going down?

165	What energizes you?
166	When do you need different pacing than what your usual pacing is?
167	What is deeply satisfying from the experience of being with your (coworkers/customers/_____)?
168	How do you best take part in your work?
169	What are the environments that bring out the best in you?
170	When do you feel most energetic and fulfilled at work?

Fear

171	What are your concerns about that the (culture/growth plans/_____)?
172	What could get in your way to achieve your (mission/dreams/_____)?
173	What is scary about the new (roles/responsibilities/_____) for you?
174	What concerns, fears, and/or questions do you have when setting goals for yourself?
175	What most upsets you about your (work/role/_____)?
176	How can you avoid being discouraged often due to fear or lack of faith in yourself?
177	What is becoming clearer about your place in the company?
178	Where are you allowing your inner critic to run the show?

Feelings

179	Whether you are setting goals or just defining a sense of direction, what will it feel like when you reach them?
180	What do you need to do to be more (empathetic/understanding/_____) towards others?
181	How can you become more aware of what is contributing to your feelings?
182	How do you feel about (change/stress/_____)?
183	How does your (team/manager/_____) make you feel?
184	What is your attitude towards (work/goal setting/_____)?
185	What is your mood towards your current (work/performance/_____)?
186	What is significant for you about today?

187	How would you feel if you can get a (promotion/job transfer/_____)?
188	What are you feeling as you face the (situation/challenge/_____)?
189	What are you feeling as you learn about your (opportunities for improvement/potential/_____)?
190	What does your (work/profession/_____) mean for you?
191	What is the impact of the (issue/problem/_____) on you?
192	How is your (role/team/_____) influencing your feelings or mood?

Flow

193	Where do you choose to focus primarily?
194	What is the common theme running through the things that you do well and with a sense of flow?
195	What is the 'thing' you are always motivated to do, and that shows up in all your most energizing, fulfilling experiences?
196	How can you experience more flow in your (work/responsibilities/_____)?
197	When working on a (project/task/_____), what would be the determinant for you to push forward or take some time to consolidate and integrate?
198	How does your inner- self-processing system influence how you navigate through your work?
199	What is your optimum state of being at work?
200	How can you access your optimum state more often?
201	How can you help yourself access your optimal self when dealing with your daily (responsibilities/problems/_____)?
202	Think about a specific moment in your life when you felt deeply engaged or fulfilled, what made such a moment special?

Fulfillment

203	What makes work (meaningful/boring/_____) for you?
204	Who are you?
205	Who do you want to be?
206	What does it keep you from becoming a more fully realized person?
207	What do you need to develop in yourself to be your own hero?
208	What do you need to do to become a super (boss/leader/_____)?
209	What are the things that provide you with fulfillment at work?

Goals

210	What is your most important purpose nowadays?
211	What is the first idea that comes to your mind as your professional purpose?
212	Whether you are setting goals or just defining a sense of direction, how will you know when you reach them?
213	When you reach your (learning goals/performance goals/_____) what would that give you?
214	What tends to distract you from your goals?
215	What is the goal that if you achieve it, it will make other things much easier?
216	How can you use your strengths to help you achieve your goals?

217	How might you go about achieving your goal?
218	What goals should you continue to focus on?
219	What new goals have emerged?
220	What are the most important tasks that you would like to achieve this year?
221	What do you need to achieve your (target/goals/_____)?
222	Where you are now relative to what you want to achieve?
223	What is the learning goal that will move you closer to achieving your performance goal?
224	When you reach your fulfillment goals, what will you have?

225	What goals would you like to set?
226	What is next for you in terms of development?
227	What do you really want to achieve?
228	What kind of accomplishment do you want for your future?

Habits

229	What do you consistently end up (doing/thinking/_____) no matter what the context is?
230	What (role/task/_____) do you consistently seem to be attracted to independently of the environment?
231	What would you like to try next to reduce your (errors/miscalculations/_____) in your reports?
232	What external obstacles could impede your targeted (deliverables/cash flows/_____)?
233	How might you get in your own way to become a more fulfilled (professional/leader/_____)?
234	How can you broaden your current (perspective/thinking pattern/_____)?
235	What is a recurrent pattern in your career?

236	What habits do you need to (change/improve/_____) at work?
237	When do you stop listening to your (colleagues/clients /_____)?
238	What is the impact if you are fully present when compared when not fully present?
239	What do you feel would make your work more effective?

Learning

240	What are you learning about (yourself/your team/_____)?
241	What are you taking away from the experience?
242	What would be the reason for your energy going down?
243	What does not work well and that could be a significantly missed opportunity?
244	How can you keep exploring and connecting your thoughts to counteract the inner critic that shuts you down?
245	How is that shaping your beliefs and assumptions?
246	Are you aware of what did not work well?
247	What is a significant missed opportunity in the last year?

248	Do you have a sense of how you would do it "better" if you could have again the opportunity?
249	What are you now curious about?
250	What are you learning about yourself as you progress in your (role/project/_____)?
251	What are you seeking now to grow yourself?
252	What did you learn about the (situation/project/_____) that worked?
253	What did you learn about the (situation/project/_____) that didn't work?
254	What can you learn about your (colleagues/clients/_____)?
255	What would be a learning opportunity related to your (performance/work/_____)?

256	What would be some of the critical variables that you think may be useful to observe when you (work/contribute/_____) with others?
257	What can you learn about yourself from a successful (priority/task/_____)?
258	What have you learned from previous (roles/projects/_____)?
259	What was the missed opportunity?
260	What has worked well for you when working with your (team/supervisor/_____)?
261	What has been least beneficial?
262	What else would you like to learn?
263	How have your (failures/successes/_____) contributed to your duties and work?

264	What are the new areas in your professional life where you want to become more effective?
265	What has been the biggest lesson from a recent (success/failure/_____) in your professional life?
266	What was a great lesson that you learned in a tough moment in your professional life?
267	What did you learn from the last time that you fail?
268	What was something that you sacrificed that has given something even better?
269	What has (surprised/challenged/_____) you recently?
270	What did you learn from something that has challenged you recently?
271	What was a situation in your life where you wish you could have done something differently?

272	What did you learn from a situation in your life where you wish you should have done something differently?
273	When can you find more insights about (yourself/purpose/_____)?
274	What has been one of the most positive learning experiences about yourself at work?
275	What did you do right when you faced a challenge where you took a risk and it paid off?

Listening

276	What kind of conversation would you have with yourself to move the (acquisition/project/_____) forward?
277	What is the missed opportunity when you don't do your best at work?
278	What failures did you experience on the pathway to those successes?
279	What impedes (listening/helping/_____) others?
280	How can you better help yourself identify where you are most stuck in a (project/problem/_____)?
281	How can you get better at listening?
282	How can you prevent harmless things affect you in the future?

Mindset

283	What is there for you to appreciate about (successes/failures/_____)?
284	How is your own state affecting the relationships with your (supervisor/subordinate/_____)?
285	How does your (work/environment/_____) might limit you?
286	What is stopping you from acting on your own (priorities/ideas/_____) now?
287	What are your criteria for (success/failure/_____)?
288	How well do your (beliefs/mindset/_____) serve you?
289	What mindset are you choosing for you today?
290	What questions can you ask yourself to raise awareness of the mindset you are operating with?

291	What are the conditions in which you feel most comfortable (at work/when working with colleagues/_____)?
292	What are the conditions in which you feel most vulnerable (at work/when working with colleagues/_____)?
293	What are you more curious about your (work/team members/_____)?
294	How will you feed your curiosity?
295	What is possible in your role?
296	Where would you rather be than in your current position?
297	What is unique about the (opportunity/role/_____) you have?
298	Who are you professionally at your best?

299	What if you really believe that you could change your results by changing your choices?
300	What are you actively pursuing in your profession?
301	What do you most want from the (experience/challenge/_____)?
302	What are you trying to accomplish?
303	What purpose is being served when you are trying to accomplish the goals of your (team/company/_____)?
304	How can you encourage more of your self-observation?
305	What are you prepared to do to move forward?
306	How do you best survive in difficult times?

Options

307	What are your choices to deal with a potential (bankruptcy/economic crisis/_____)?
308	What is your choice right now?
309	How will you approach the (obstacle/goal/_____)?
310	What do you see as the opportunities in the (project/problem/_____)?
311	How will you approach the (problem/meeting/_____) if you see it as an opportunity?
312	What is another perspective on the (plan/commitment/_____)?
313	What is right about the (experience/project/_____)?
314	What new possibilities do you see for improving the (situation/task/_____)?

315	What is more important for you between stability and challenge?
316	What will make the biggest difference in the (project/plan/_____)?
317	What options appeal to you?
318	What prompted the choice of selecting your current (role/position/_____)?
319	What has been working when you make your choices?
320	What hasn't been working when you make your choices?
321	What would you like to improve about (yourself/your team/_____)?

Performance

322	What resulted from your efforts on your (top priorities/goals/_____) last year?
323	How have your results on (team projects/tasks/_____) moved you forward professionally?
324	What did it lead up to the (budget deficit/closure/_____) of your department?
325	How do you feel when you do your best work?
326	What would be an ideal outcome for (you/your business/_____)?
327	How can you facilitate change in yourself that will lead to your desired (results/performance/_____)?
328	How could you overcome what is blocking you from your potential?
329	What can you do (better/faster/_____)?

330	What do you commit to doing to improve your (relationships/performance/_____)?
331	What goal, if not acted on, might have the biggest negative impact?
332	What does need to be (different/change/_____) for you to achieve your performance goals?
333	What do you feel you have most benefited from working here?
334	What would the process to improving your (performance/results/_____) look like?
335	What are you most proud of?
336	What values can guide your own development toward realizing your potential?

Preferences

337	What do you pay attention to?
338	How do you choose what to pay attention to?
339	How do you define (success/failure/_____)?
340	What do you like about your (work/role/_____)?
341	What would you do if you knew you had very limited time left?

Priorities

342	What do you need to stop doing to be more productive?
343	What is your experience of managing multiple (priorities/goals/_____) at the same time?
344	What is your highest priority at work?
345	How will you prioritize your goals in relation to the others you have been working on?
346	What is most important to you about the (company/company's culture/_____)?
347	What is the priority now?
348	What do you really want?

Progress

349	What does (winning/progress/_____) mean to you?
350	What does need to change to improve your (well-being/mental health/_____) at work?
351	What signposts do you recognize in your own (learning/change/_____) process?
352	How can you celebrate your successes?
353	What are the possibilities when you do your best?
354	How are you different now as compared to when you started working with the company?
355	What steps are involved when you set plans for (success/improvement/_____)?
356	What can you put in place to track your (progress/performance/_____)?

357	How do you feel about your progress when trying to reach for your (goals/targets/_____)?
358	How satisfied are you with your pace of progress?
359	What are the best ways you can stay on the path to your development?
360	What is one accomplishment that you are very proud of working hard to achieve?

Purpose

361	When you reflect on your professional life, what's the recurring theme or common thread?
362	What is your vision for yourself with the (company/team/_____)?
363	What do you now better understand about your (purpose/priorities/_____)?
364	What is essential to you about 'being on purpose'?
365	What is the emotional connection with your purpose?
366	What do you want to achieve with your team?
367	What is the (goal/objective/_____) you'd like to achieve?
368	How will you know when you achieve your intention?

369	What will you do if you fail in achieving your (desirable targets/goals/_____)?
370	What are you willing to do?
371	What do you want?
372	Who do you want to be?
373	What do you want to have?
374	What contribution do you want to make to the (company/team/_____)?
375	What is your purpose?
376	Where are you on purpose?
377	What gives you a sense of purpose in your (work/career/_____)?
378	What do you understand now about your purpose?

Relationships

379	How have your recent (successes/failures/_____) affected others?
380	What is important to you about the support from your (leader/manager/_____)?
381	Whose responsibility is the (project/task/_____)?
382	What brings you fulfillment when working with (colleagues/clients/_____)?
383	What could be your contribution to creating more trusting, open relationships with (suppliers/clients/_____)?
384	How can you find out what works well in interactions with others?
385	How do you frame your duties in relation to the rest of your team?
386	How can you develop supportive and trusting relationships with your (colleagues/clients/_____)?

387	What are you learning about yourself in your relationship with others?
388	What types of people are you drawn to?
389	What is it for you to be fully present and fully yourself with (others/clients/_____)?
390	Where do you give away your power in relationships?
391	What is the nature or quality of your presence when you are fully present?
392	What is the nature or quality of your presence when you are not present?
393	What gets in the way of you being fully present?
394	What are the triggers that typically have you "shrink back" in an interaction?

395	How do you best contribute to your team?
396	What is important about being with your (team/colleagues/_____)?
397	What is important to you about sparking ideas with others?
398	Who else needs to be involved?
399	In what way do others need to be involved?
400	How will you involve others?
401	What would be your advice to a colleague who is concerned about you?
402	What is a relationship at work that you should improve?
403	What would be the first step you should take towards improving the relationship with your (client/colleague/_____)?

404	What kind of quality of a career you would like others to have from you?
405	What do you bring to relationships with (clients/colleagues/_____)?
406	What would you choose to do if you wanted to be an active and contributing member of the (team/company/_____)?

407	What does support you in being fully present at team meetings?
408	What fuels your passion for work?
409	What resources you could access to face any obstacles at work in a more fulfilled way?
410	What support or resources do you need to do your work better?
411	How can you help yourself develop long-term resourcefulness?
412	What resources do you have available to help yourself move forward?
413	What structures do you need to put in place to have more patience with yourself?
414	What new (habits/behaviors/_____) will support you best?

415	How can be developed or changed to serve you better?
416	How can you become more aware of your (feelings/emotions/_____) that are involved in the situation you are exploring?
417	What tools do you need to develop to give yourself the confidence to better deal with your (responsibilities/targets/_____)?
418	How can you access your own power to create the career you want for yourself?
419	What does it take for you to access your self-trust?
420	What tools do you have to inspire yourself?
421	When you notice you are not being fully present, how can you bring yourself back?
422	What contributes to meaningful (responsibilities/roles/_____)?

423	What resources could you access to assist with your work?
424	What resources do you need to better support your (team/manager/_____)?
425	What are your most precious resources?
426	How can you use your current resources for whatever you are now facing?
427	What structures do you have available to help you?
428	What would you do if you had unlimited time and resources?

Self-Assessment

429	What did lead you to say your (comments/accusations/_____)?
430	How will you take the first step to improve (professionally/your presentations skills/_____)?
431	When will you take the first step to improve (professionally/your presentations skills/_____)?
432	Where you are now relative to where you want to be professionally?
433	Who are you at your core?
434	What makes you unique?
435	What are you passionate about?
436	What professional (successes/failures/_____) have you experienced recently?

437	What did you learn from recent (successes/failures/_____)?
438	How has your perspective on your (responsibilities/potential/_____) changed over time?
439	How can you be more self-observant?
440	How can you gain a deeper insight into what you desire for the future?
441	How will you measure progress?
442	What is truly essential to you in your (work/company/_____)?
443	What took for you to accomplish the one thing that you are most proud of?

Skills

444	What is the gap in your skills between your current reality and your desired future?
445	What new skills do you need to add in order to reach your (performance indicators/cost reduction targets/_____)?
446	What skills energize and inspire you as you use them?
447	How have the skills that energize and inspire you changed over the years?
448	What is the best route for you to gain a new skill?
449	Where is your highest leverage?
450	What are new skills you want to become more effective in?
451	What skills do you already have that you can use in pursuit of your (goals/key performance indicators/_____)?
452	What are the (skills/qualities/_____) required to create collaboratively?

Strategies

453	How can you acknowledge yourself for your (courage/commitment/_____) even if you fail in your strategy?
454	What are possible strategies for achieving your (key performance indicators/cost reduction targets/_____)?
455	What could get in the way of you taking the required steps to complete your (forecast/budget/_____)?
456	How can you experiment with new (behaviors/thoughts/_____)?
457	What (strategy/plan/_____) will be easiest for you?
458	What (strategy/plan/_____) will be most effective and/or efficient?
459	What new (strategy/plan/_____) will fit in with the reality of your current situation?

Strength

460	What strengths of your come into play when you face exhilarating challenges?
461	Considering your life in the last 5 years, which are the top three to five strengths you have used in that period?
462	What comes easy to you?
463	Taking into consideration the (role/task/_____) you consistently seem to be attracted to, what does that tell you about your strengths?
464	Have your (passion/joy/_____) for using a particular strength increased or decreased over the years?
465	Is there any strength or set of strengths that feels especially right for you?
466	When you look at your list of strengths, what patterns do you see?
467	What are your inner (gifts/talents/_____)?

468	What are your strengths?
469	What are the pieces of evidence of your strengths in your career?
470	How strongly do you own your strengths?
471	What are you noticing about your own strengths?
472	How will you know when you are using a strength?
473	How do you intend to work with your strength?
474	What will be easy for you?
475	What are the assets from your past that you can leverage in the future?
476	What does it happen when you are using one of your strengths?

477	Considering your strengths in your (goals/objectives/_____), how do your strengths serve you?
478	How could you use your strengths to move you forward towards your (goals/objectives/_____)?
479	How can you learn to notice how your strengths show up in your (work/responsibilities/_____)?
480	When do you push your strengths to their extreme?
481	What is the impact when you push your strengths to the extreme?
482	How do you know when you push your strengths too far?
483	What are some unintended consequences of your strengths?
484	What is the impact of your strengths on others?
485	When are you tempted to hide your strengths under a shade?

486	What strengths do you have that you no longer enjoy using?
487	Where are you pretending a strength where there isn't one?
488	How can you leverage your strengths?
489	How good is the fit between what your (role/position/_____) requires of you and your actual strengths?
490	What is the impact of the misalignment between your role and your strengths?
491	What can you do to enhance the alignment between your role and your strengths?
492	How can you hone your strengths?
493	What opportunities do you see for practicing a specific strength?
494	When you are looking for a greater sense of fulfillment, how can you help yourself consider how you can use your strengths more in all areas of your life?

Support

495	What can you do to prevent making an incorrect (assumption/action/_____)?
496	How can you support yourself to stay focused on the (big picture/task/_____)?
497	What can you do to provide yourself with a self-confidence boost?
498	What will move you forward towards desired (results/sales/_____)?
499	What structures does the company need to put in place to support (you/your work/_____)?
500	What support do you need to have available to have more patience with your (suppliers/customers/_____)?
501	What do you need to let go of in order to move forward more powerfully?
502	How can you put in place a new habit that will support you to achieve better (workflow/results/_____)?

503	What alternative to your current (work schedule/work environment/_____) can be constructed that would serve you better?
504	How can you better support your own (creativity/well-being/_____)?
505	What structures can you put in place to help you achieve the (project/goals/_____)?
506	What do you need to have to ensure you can move the (project/team/_____) forward?
507	What support do you need to pursue your next new (client/employee/_____)?
508	What will you do to get the support you need?
509	What support do you need to take the first step?
510	How can you help yourself deal with disappointment?
511	What is a challenge in your professional life where a new structure is needed?

Values

512	What do you value most in your profession?
513	What do you value in your (work/team/_____)?
514	What are the values of the (company/team/_____) that represent you?
515	What values anchor you in who you are?
516	What values can guide your development towards realizing your potential?
517	What values guide you in creating and maintaining meaningful and productive relationships with (colleagues/clients/_____)?
518	What is the most radical step you can take to honor your values more fully?
519	What can you change to honor your values more?

520	What small action can you take to be more in line with your values?
521	What are your values?
522	Where are you honoring your values?
523	Where are you not honoring your values?
524	How can you use your values to make better choices?
525	How can you use your values to design a fulfilling way towards a (goal/objective/_____)?
526	What are the values and guiding principles that help you shed light on challenges?
527	How else can your values be honored?

528	What is it costing you to continue ignoring your values?
529	What is one small step you could take to live more of your values?
530	What are the reasons for the importance of what you value?
531	What is the relative order of importance of your values?
532	What values were you honoring in a moment in your life when you felt deeply (engaged/fulfilled/_____)?
533	What does it mean for you to act on what matters, given your personal values?
534	What values can guide you in creating and maintaining meaningful and productive relationships?

Weakness

535	What are the gaps in your (skills/knowledge/_____)?
536	What is the impact of your weaknesses on your work?
537	What weaknesses do you need to work on to help you achieve your goals?
538	How strongly do you own your weaknesses?
539	Where can you leverage your (weaknesses/strengths/_____)?
540	What are your (weaknesses/gaps/_____)?
541	How can you give up familiar habits that generate fear and anxiety?
542	How do your weaknesses get you into trouble?

543	What is the impact when you don't improve your weaknesses?
544	What are some unintended consequences of your weaknesses?
545	What blind spots could you be missing?
546	What are your weaknesses?
547	What is the evidence of your weakness in your (career/performance/_____)?
548	When do you consider your non-strengths, which ones do you suspect will have a pay-off for you if you were to enhance them?
549	How do you know what kinds of weaknesses you are dealing with?
550	What is costing you from not working on your weaknesses?

551	Where are you pretending a weakness, where there is strength?
552	What will it mean to you if you can become really masterful at a current weakness you might have?
553	What can you learn or practice that will make you better at a certain weakness?
554	What (skill/competence/_____) do you need to gain?
555	What internal qualities do you need to grow and enhance your performance?

FREE PERSONALITY TESTS

✐ Principles You

QR CODE:

📄 Test Duration: 15-20 minutes.

📄 Test Description: Designed to help gain self-awareness and others' awareness that are critical to making excellent decisions and getting things done.

✐ 16 Personality Test

QR CODE:

📄 Test Duration: 10 minutes.

📄 Test Description: - Based on the work of famous Swiss psychiatrist Carl Jung.

📄 What it tests: The 16 Types test is like the Myers Briggs Type Indicator, because it tells us where a candidate gets their energy, how they process information, how they decide, and what type of lifestyle they prefer.

🖉 Disc Personality Testing

📄 Test Duration: 10 minutes.

📄 Test Description: - The DISC test is based on the model developed by psychologist William Marston for behavioral assessment. It classifies how we express emotions into the four behavior types of DISC: dominance (D), influence (I), steadiness (S), and conscientiousness (C).

QR CODE:

🖉 Enneagram Test

📄 Test Duration: 10 minutes.

📄 Test Description: The Enneagram personality test is based on work by Oscar Ichazo and Claudio Naranjo. It posits that there are nine unique personality types that can capture someone's core belief system or worldview. The Enneagram results give you insight into how the candidate is likely to approach interpersonal relationships in the workplace.

QR CODE:

✏ High5Test

📄 Test Duration: 15-20 minutes.

📄 Test Description: HIGH 5 Test is a free strengths test helping people to discover their unique talents and to live a life full of happiness and fulfillment.

QR CODE:

✏ Big 5 Personality Test

📄 Test Duration: 5-10 minutes.

📄 Test Description: The Big Five personality test measures the five personality factors that psychologists have determined are core to our personality makeup. The Five Factors of personality

QR CODE:

are: (1) Openness; (2) Extraversion; (30 Agreeableness; (4) Neuroticism.

📄 The Big Five model of personality is widely considered being the most scientifically robust way to describe personality differences. It is the basis of most modern personality research.

Made in United States
Troutdale, OR
06/05/2024

20343208R00061